# DO PENGUINS LIKE THE COLD?

**HUW LEWIS JONES**

EXPEDITION LEADER

**SAM CALDWELL**

WILDLIFE ARTIST

# CONTENTS

# EXPEDITION PENGUIN!

## What do you know about penguins?

Are you a bird nerd like me? I hope so. Join us on an epic adventure—we'll navigate to distant islands, through big seas, and around dangerous icebergs to find penguins in their wild environments.

Can you imagine being a penguin? Freezing all day long and only eating fish for dinner? You'd have to really like the cold, right? Well, on this voyage you'll discover why penguins love where they live, how they survive, and what we can do to protect them and their natural homes, or habitats.

## Summer fun

During the winter in Antarctica, the surface of the ocean all around the continent freezes solid! Not only that, but there are also months of total darkness. That's why we're heading south in the summer rather than the winter— so we can see what we're looking at!

## Super cold

Just how cold might it get on our voyage? Well, the coldest temperature ever recorded in Antarctica is -128.6°F! We'll be finding penguins near the coasts, where it is a little warmer than that, but it's still freezing by human standards.

## What do I need?

A brave heart and warm clothes! We'll meet penguins from all over the southern hemisphere, but to begin our expedition, we're heading to Antarctica. You'll need waterproof boots, snow goggles, and a good hat. Remember to bring a journal for drawing and writing observations. And don't forget a canteen for your hot chocolate!

# SEARCHING FOR BIRDS

## Would you like to meet a penguin?

Penguins look a bit funny and out of place on land, walking clumsily and often falling over as they move across the snow. But once you see their skill and grace shooting through the water, you'll know that's where they're meant to be. Penguins split their time between land and sea, and are perfectly adapted to life in the ocean.

### What does "penguin" mean?

The origin of the word "penguin" still has people arguing. Some think it comes from Welsh sailors who saw similar birds and called them *pen gwyn*, or "white head," for the white patches on their heads. Others say it comes from the Latin *pinguis*, which means "fat."

## FIELD NOTES: ADÉLIE PENGUIN

**LOCATION**
Antarctica, South Georgia, and the South Sandwich Islands

**HABITAT**
Ice and islands

**HEIGHT**
35 inches

**FOOT COLOR**
Pink

**FAVORITE SNACK**
Krill and small fish

## Bird words

Most penguins like to live together in big groups called colonies. When they swim together at sea, they sometimes gather on the surface—this is called a raft of penguins. And when they move together on the land, it is sometimes called a waddle of penguins. It's easy to see why when they walk!

## Learn to love

Humans haven't always been kind to penguins—in the past people caught them to eat and to use their fat, oil, and feathers. Famous explorers like Captain Scott even had them roasted for Christmas dinner! Thankfully, it's now illegal to hunt or kill penguins. There are two simple things we can do to help penguins. Firstly, we can respect them in nature, and secondly, we can do everything in our power to protect their ice-and-ocean habitat.

# THE ENDS OF THE EARTH

## Where do penguins live?

When we think about penguins, most of us think of Antarctica—it has the biggest penguin population out there. But did you know penguins also live in Angola, Argentina, Australia, Chile, Namibia, New Zealand, and South Africa, not to mention on all sorts of smaller islands?

← NOT A PENGUIN

← ANTARCTICA

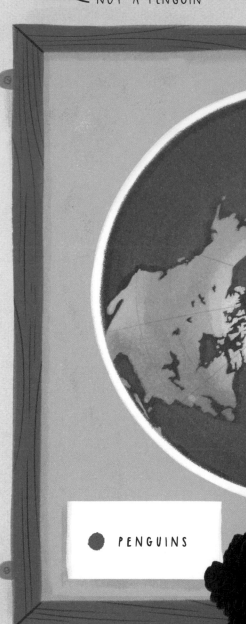

● PENGUINS

### Where on Earth?

You might be thinking, *where on Earth is Antarctica?!* Well, we're starting our voyage at very the bottom of the globe. Antarctica is an amazing frozen continent in the far south. It's one of the coldest, windiest, and wildest places on our beautiful planet.

8

### Don't get lost

The rare Galápagos penguins live on the Galápagos Islands. They are the most northerly species of penguin and we will meet them on our adventures too. They are the only penguins that sometimes swim into the northern hemisphere.

## Polar extremes

There are no penguins in the Arctic, which is that huge region at the top of a standard world map. There are many other amazing seabirds there, though, like guillemots, puffins, and razorbills. These three species are all black and white and look a bit like penguins!

## Ahoy there!

While the most well-known penguins live in freezing Antarctica, different species live in different habitats, from ice to rocky coasts, sandy beaches, and even forest floors. One thing they have in common is that nearly all of them live in the southern hemisphere.

# KNOW YOUR PENGUINS

## What makes a penguin a penguin?

Just a few hundred years ago, when European explorers first saw penguins, some thought they might be feathered fish! Penguins are *so* good at swimming. When they race through the water near the surface, they sometimes jump into the air, a little like a dolphin. But they are definitely *not* fish, or mammals for that matter! Penguins are birds and proud of it.

### Birds of a feather

Penguins are unusual birds. They never perch in trees (there are no trees in Antarctica)! They spend a lot of time at sea. And what about the most bird-like thing of all, flying? Well, penguins can't fly! But we will soon find out they have lots of cool skills, so that doesn't bother them at all.

## Brilliant beak

A penguin's beak (also known as a bill) is its most important tool. Penguins use it to catch and hold slippery fish. Penguins have no teeth, so they have to swallow their food whole!

## Big-headed bird

Penguins have large heads that they hunch into their shoulders when they swim. This makes them more streamlined.

## Flipping heck!

Penguins have wings that are called flippers. Their flippers are flat and streamlined, which means they are perfectly designed to help them swim fast.

## Secret stilts

Penguins have surprisingly long legs hidden under their amazing feathery bodies. They don't really kick with their feet when swimming, but they use the position of their feet to steer—it's kind of like changing the position of the handlebars on a bike to change direction. Penguins are less skilled at walking on land, which is what gives them their famous waddle.

## Preen machine

Penguins regularly comb and clean their feathers. When they do this, they use their beaks to coat their feathers in a waxy oil. This is known as preening. The oil comes from the "preen gland," an organ near the bottom of a penguin's back. This oil makes their feathers waterproof, moisturizes them and might even help to prevent infections.

## How many different penguins are there?

There are eighteen different kinds—or species—of penguin in the wild. The different species are all unique. The eighteen penguin species can be grouped together into six different categories, or genuses. They are all part of the same animal family, which scientists call the *Spheniscidae*.

## IUCN Red List

Scientists are keeping a careful watch over all the penguins in the world to make sure they're safe. Look for this symbol to see which species are most in need of our help.

## Spheniscus genus:
# THE BANDED OR JACKASS PENGUINS

**HUMBOLDT PENGUIN:**
HOW MANY? 24,000
STATUS: Vulnerable

**MAGELLANIC PENGUIN:**
HOW MANY? 3 million
STATUS: Least concern

**GALÁPAGOS PENGUIN:**
HOW MANY? 1,200
STATUS: Endangered

**AFRICAN PENGUIN:**
HOW MANY? 42,000
STATUS: Endangered

## Megadyptes genus:
# THE LARGE DIVER PENGUINS

**YELLOW-EYED PENGUIN (ALSO KNOWN AS HOIHO):**
HOW MANY? 4,000
STATUS: Endangered

## Eudyptula genus:
# THE LITTLE DIVER PENGUINS

**LITTLE PENGUIN (ALSO KNOWN AS KORORĀ):**
HOW MANY? 470,000
STATUS: Least concern

## Aptenodytes genus:
# THE GREAT PENGUINS

**EMPEROR PENGUIN:**
HOW MANY? 500,000
STATUS: Near threatened

**KING PENGUIN:**
HOW MANY? 2 million
STATUS: Least concern

*Pygoscelis genus:*
# THE BRUSH-TAILED PENGUINS

**CHINSTRAP PENGUIN:**
HOW MANY? 8 million
STATUS: Least concern

**ADÉLIE PENGUIN:**
HOW MANY? 10 million
STATUS: Least concern

**GENTOO PENGUIN:**
HOW MANY? 776,000
STATUS: Least concern

*Eudyptes genus:*
# THE CRESTED PENGUINS

**SNARES PENGUIN:**
HOW MANY? 60,000
STATUS: Vulnerable

**NORTHERN ROCKHOPPER PENGUIN:**
HOW MANY? 400,000, but numbers are falling rapidly
STATUS: Endangered

**MACARONI PENGUIN:**
HOW MANY? 12 million, but numbers are falling rapidly
STATUS: Vulnerable

**ERECT-CRESTED PENGUIN:**
IIOW MANY? 150,000, but numbers are falling rapidly
STATUS: Endangered

**FIORDLAND PENGUIN:**
HOW MANY? 30,000
STATUS: Vulnerable

**SOUTHERN ROCKHOPPER PENGUIN:**
HOW MANY? 2.5 million
STATUS: Vulnerable

**ROYAL PENGUIN:**
HOW MANY? 1.7 million
STATUS: Near threatened

# PREHISTORIC PARTY

## Were there dino-penguins?

Long before humans, there were all sorts of weird and wonderful creatures on Earth. Though penguins aren't dinosaurs, they have been around for almost as long! Finding fossils in the ground has helped researchers learn more about animal history. Fossils of the very earliest penguins tell us they emerged around the time dinosaurs roamed the Earth.

## Survivors

Long ago, an asteroid smashed into the Earth and wiped out the big dinosaurs and many other predators. When that happened, the early penguins thrived. At first, they lived in warm waters, but over time some ventured further south in search of food and breeding places. Eventually, they evolved in a wide variety of shapes and sizes.

## The first penguins

The earliest fossils of penguins date to around 62 million years ago. They were found in New Zealand. That very first penguin species is known as *Waimanu*—the name comes from the Māori words *wai* and *manu*, meaning "water bird."

### ICADYPTES

**HEIGHT:** Almost 5 ft

**WEIGHT:** 110–176 lbs

**WHERE:** The coastal deserts of Peru

**WHEN:** About 36 million years ago

### MODERN DAY GALÁPAGOS PENGUIN

**HEIGHT:** 20 inches

**WEIGHT:** 3.5–5.5 lbs

**WHERE:** Galápagos Islands, Ecuador

**WHEN:** Now

## ANTHROPORNIS

**HEIGHT:** About 5.9 feet (that's almost twice as big as an emperor penguin!)

**WEIGHT:** About 200 lbs

**WHERE:** Antarctica and New Zealand

**WHEN:** About 40 million years ago

## PACHYDYPTES

**HEIGHT:** About 5 ft

**WEIGHT:** The big daddy of them all—maybe over 220 lbs!

**WHERE:** New Zealand

**WHEN:** About 35 million years ago

## March of the giant penguins

Giant prehistoric penguins? Sounds like something out of a movie, but it's true! Some ancient penguins reached up to almost 6 feet tall and might have weighed more than 220 lbs. That's about as heavy as a giant panda or baby elephant!

# FISHY FEAST

## What do penguins eat?

Penguins are carnivores. Their food comes entirely from the sea: fish, squid, crabs, and krill. In general, penguins aren't picky, and they'll eat what they can catch. When hunting, a penguin swims beneath fish and uses its buoyancy (ability to float) to shoot up and catch them. It surprises its prey—kind of like a lion pouncing from the long grass, but under water!

## Fishy diet

Some king penguins love herring, while Galápagos penguins eat mullet. Humboldt penguins enjoy sardines, and big emperor penguins eat lantern fish from the deep sea. Some penguins even eat pebbles! Scientists think they help penguins break up their food. This might be handy because penguins don't chew when they eat.

## Sharing is caring

A penguin parent eats its dinner and starts to digest it before it feeds its chick. It then throws up the partially digested food into the chick's beak! The baby eats this way until it learns to hunt and feed itself.

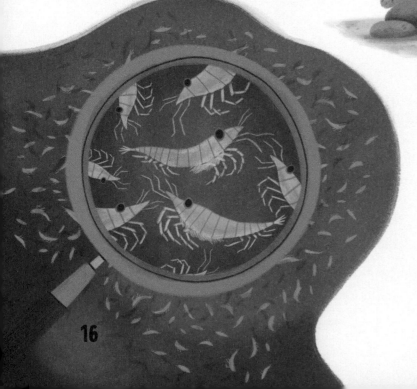

## Cool krill

Krill are small crustaceans that look a little like shrimp or prawns. The krill in the seas around Antarctica are hugely important. They are eaten by whales, seals, squid, fish, and, of course, penguins! Even though they're tiny, there are so many krill that together they would weigh more than all the humans on Earth!

## Poop collectors

Biologists collect poop from all kinds of animals to learn more about their health and behavior—and, of course, what they had for lunch! Researchers mostly call animal poop **scat**, but they also refer to it as dung, droppings, and, in the case of seabirds, guano.

## Watch out

When Adélie penguins need to use the bathroom, they shoot out a hot jet of liquid poop—which can reach up to 5 feet away! This helps them keep their nests clean, particularly when they have eggs and chicks. Not so great for their neighbors, though!

**Pink poop** usually means a penguin had krill for dinner. Adélie penguins love krill—they can eat up to 2 lbs of them every day.

**Yellow poop** usually means a penguin had squid for dinner.

**White poop** usually means a penguin had fish for dinner.

**Green poop** means a penguin hasn't had enough food and is starving.

# FLIPPER FANTASTIC

## Do penguins want to fly?

Penguins are the only flightless seabirds. Even though they can't fly in the air, they are excellent swimmers and can fly through the water at incredible speeds! Their bodies are streamlined like rockets. Penguins are so fast and sleek underwater it could look like they don't have feathers. In fact, they have up to one hundred feathers per square inch—that's more than most birds.

## Ice jump

Though penguins can't fly, many species are able to leap from the water onto the ice. Adélie penguins can jump up almost 10 feet! They squash down their feathers to release air bubbles. This helps them double or even triple their speed before they shoot into the air.

## Super speedy

Some penguins can zip through the sea almost four times as fast as an Olympic swimmer. The fastest are gentoo penguins, which can go up to 22 miles per hour in short bursts. They are also very busy feeders, sometimes making more than 400 dives each day!

## Dive down

Penguins have **evolved** so their bones help them swim. Other birds have hollow bones, which are light and good for flying, whereas penguins have solid bones. These let them sink down and swim more easily, instead of bobbing up to the surface.

## In the deep end

Emperor penguins are the record-breaking divers of the bird world—their deepest dive ever known was almost 1,900 feet. They can hold their breath for more than 20 minutes at a time. Incredible!

**FIELD NOTES:**
# EMPEROR PENGUIN

**LOCATION**
Antarctica

**HABITAT**
Sea ice

**HEIGHT**
39 inches

**FOOT COLOR**
Black

**FAVORITE SNACK**
Fish and squid

# SUPER SENSES

## Do you smell like a penguin?

Maybe your stinkiest pair of socks does . . . penguins are famously stinky! But, more importantly, *can* you smell like a penguin? Penguins can use their sense of smell to check who they're related to. That way they can make sure they don't nest up with any long-lost relatives—yuck! Some species of penguins also use their sense of smell to find prey.

## Awesome eyes

Penguins have excellent vision. Their eyes are a special shape and are protected by transparent eyelids, so they're ingeniously adapted for seeing underwater. It's like wearing perfect swimming goggles!

## Tongue-tastic

Did you know, penguins have really crazy tongues? They don't have teeth, so their tongues have lots of sharp points on them. It's a little like the edges of a comb. These spikes bend inwards so fish or squid don't slip away. Penguins can't taste bitterness or sweetness, they can only taste sourness and saltiness!

## Never lost

Penguins don't need maps like us. They have an amazing sense of direction! Scientists don't know exactly how, but some penguins swim hundreds of miles—or even migrate—following fish and ocean currents. But penguins are always able to find their way back to the beaches they grew up on, and find their partners among thousands of other birds.

## Night swimming

Much of a penguin's life is spent hunting for food at sea—often at night. They find their way using their super senses, though scientists don't yet fully understand how. Deep divers like emperor penguins hunt so far under water that it must be almost totally dark because they are so far from the surface. But that doesn't stop them from catching fish and squid and then finding their way home.

# TWEET THAT

## Can you speak penguin?

Are you ready to communicate? Penguins use many secret methods to talk to each other, including noises and gestures. Scientists don't know what all of these mean just yet, but they make perfect sense to other penguins! Penguins send three main types of message:

1) Simple contact sounds, like "Hello, is that you?"

2) Territorial sounds, like "I want this spot all for myself. Beat it!"

3) Bonding sounds, like "I'm into you—do you like me too?"

## No quacks allowed

Penguins make many sounds. Each has its own unique voice. They don't quack like a duck or hoot like an owl, though. Some bray like donkeys, others honk like geese, and some even growl like dogs. Many penguins "gak," which sounds like a cross between a squawk and a car engine starting!

## Baby talk

When an adult penguin returns from the sea to its colony, it can't rely on sight alone to find its partner or baby. Sometimes thousands of penguins are chatting and squabbling, arguing with their neighbors or calling for their family. Still, adult penguins can recognize the screech of their own chicks even among the noisy crowds.

## Tough guy

When king penguins defend their territory, they try to scare other males away by pointing with their flippers and staring fiercely. If their warnings don't work, they will waddle over and fight them—sometimes even beating them up with their flippers. Yikes!

## Really attractive

When males want to attract a female, they stand up tall, with their necks and flippers outstretched, braying loudly. Chinstrap penguins bob their heads up and down and make all kinds of noises!

# CROWD CONTROL

## Do penguins get lonely?

Most penguins enjoy hanging out with other penguins. Though they argue and sometimes get into fights, they are generally very sociable. All but two species breed in large colonies, ranging from a few hundred to hundreds of thousands of birds. Colonies are safer and also offer the chance for penguins to share knowledge about where the best fish are.

## Taking turns

Penguins often huddle together for warmth and to shelter from the wind. In colonies of emperor penguins, the males will regularly shuffle around so everyone gets a turn to be warm in the middle of the group.

## Largest colony

The largest penguin colony in the world is on Zavodovski Island in the southern Atlantic Ocean. More than 2 million chinstrap penguins breed there at the edge of an active volcano! Chinstraps get their name from a thin, curved line of black feathers under their chin, which looks kind of like a helmet strap.

### FIELD NOTES:
### CHINSTRAP PENGUIN

**LOCATION**
Antarctica and islands including Bouvet and South Georgia

**HABITAT**
Rocks and cliffs

**HEIGHT**
25 inches

**FOOT COLOR**
Pink

**FAVORITE SNACK**
Shrimp, squid, small fish

## Marvelous macaroni!

The world's most plentiful penguin species is the macaroni penguin, a crested penguin found on many islands and the Antarctic Peninsula. There are more than 12 million macaronis, which is a lot! But the IUCN are concerned because macaroni numbers have been falling since the 1970s.

## Least social

Meanwhile, yellow-eyed penguins really *don't* like crowds! They prefer to nest alone. They don't mind the sound of other birds, but they prefer to hide away in flax scrub and forest. Their nests are usually shallow bowls filled with twigs and grass.

## FIELD NOTES:
## MACARONI PENGUIN

**LOCATION**
Antarctica and surrounding islands

**HABITAT**
Rocks and cliffs

**HEIGHT**
24 inches

**FOOT COLOR**
Pink

**FAVORITE SNACK**
Krill

# COOL SKILLS

## Do penguins like the cold?

Most penguins love the cold, and have evolved to survive in freezing climates. But some penguins never even see snow! The "banded" penguins—Magellanic, Humboldt, Galápagos, and African penguins—live in South America and South Africa. They would probably not be able to survive the really low temperatures of Antarctica.

## Too hot to handle

Banded penguins sometimes hide away to beat the heat. They make burrows and seek shade under bushes. They can also cool off in the sea. Even though their home countries in South America and South Africa are much warmer than Antarctica, the sea is still very cold because of deep-water currents.

## Mega Magellanic

Magellanic penguins often hang out in groups at the water's edge in South America. They are amazing hunters and strong swimmers who can survive at sea for 5 months at a time. They have also been found to migrate more than 3,000 miles.

## FIELD NOTES: GALÁPAGOS PENGUIN

**LOCATION**
Galápagos Islands

**HABITAT**
Rocky beaches

**HEIGHT**
20 inches

**FOOT COLOR**
Black

**FAVORITE SNACK**
Mullet and sardines

## Keeping cool

The sun at the equator is very strong. Galápagos penguins spend a lot of time in the water during the day, which helps them keep cool. When back on land, they sometimes hold their flippers over their feet to stop them from getting sunburned!

## Frostbite

How cold is too cold for a penguin? It's hard to say, but if a penguin is weak, injured, or hungry it will struggle in really cold temperatures—especially if it's looking after an egg or chick. Many penguins spend the winter fishing at sea without coming back to land at all. It is often warmer in the sea than it is when standing out on the ice in fierce winds.

## Warming oceans

Meanwhile, the big problem for penguins in Antarctica is that the world continues to get hotter. Penguins depend on many fish that cannot survive in warm seas. As the oceans warm, these fish disappear. Penguins will have to find new places to live and hunt.

# HAPPY FEET

## Do penguins really dance?

Penguins don't stand still all day long. Sometimes, it looks like they are dancing. Well, not quite dancing, but definitely wiggling! Penguins move to adjust their temperature, to communicate, and maybe even just for fun—who really knows? They might do a slip-hop-tumble-wobble across soft snow, or jump high as they climb rocks. Some even slide across land on their bellies. It's called tobogganing!

## Shake it off

When penguins shake their heads, it is most likely to shake out salt from their special supraorbital gland. This gland in their beak helps them remove salt from their bodies. With its help, they can drink seawater safely and then shake the salt right out.

## In a flap

Penguins flap and shake their wings quite often. This could mean they are angry with a neighbor or—quite the opposite—they want to attract the attention of a potential mate.

## FIELD NOTES:
## GENTOO PENGUIN

**LOCATION**
Antarctica and surrounding islands

**HABITAT**
Rocky islands

**FOOT COLOR**
Orange

**HEIGHT**
25 inches

**FAVORITE SNACK**
Krill and small fish

## Friendly waddle

When I take people to see penguins in the wild, they are always amazed at how curious penguins are. Their main predators are in the sea so, in Antarctica at least, penguins have no fear of humans. In fact, they find us very interesting. Penguins often waddle right up and, if you stand really still, they might check you out by pecking at your boots.

## It must be love

Penguins will wave their heads, nod and bow when they want to impress a new mate. They also sing and dance, which helps them recognize or get to know each other.

## Anti-freeze

Feathers and fat keep penguins' bodies warm—but their feet are naked! Luckily, clever circulation means penguins control how much blood goes to their feet, so they stay warm enough to avoid frostbite. Still, penguins do get chilly. You can sometimes see emperor penguins rocking on their heels to keep their feet off the ice.

# URBAN ECOLOGY

## Do penguins live in cities?

Did you know that not all penguins live in remote places? In fact, some can be found very close to busy cities. Little penguins, for example, are a big hit down under, where they are spotted in some rather unlikely places. They are known as kororā in New Zealand, and fairy penguins in Australia. These wonderful little guys have blue feathers and are about the size of a bowling pin!

## Neighborhood penguins

Near Sydney in Australia, not far from the water's edge, lives a very secret colony of little penguins. They nest in burrows under decking and in bushes near people's houses. How lucky to have a penguin hiding in your backyard!

## Surf's up

Some people have even spotted penguins at Sydney's Bondi Beach! Surfers sometimes see them shooting through the waves.

### FIELD NOTES:
### LITTLE PENGUIN

**LOCATION**
New Zealand, southern Australia

**HABITAT**
Beaches and scrub

**HEIGHT**
12 inches

**FOOT COLOR**
Pink

**FAVORITE SNACK**
Anchovies, sprats, shrimp

## Nightlife

There is a colony of about 1,400 little penguins at the St Kilda breakwater near Melbourne, Australia. They are very shy, and they like darkness because it helps them avoid predators. They come ashore at dusk and make a moonlight scramble to the safety of their nesting holes. After resting overnight, they hop down from their safe spots among the rocks to go fishing once again.

## Sunset show

In the town of Oamaru in New Zealand, crowds of tourists gather to watch the penguins return home from their day of fishing. The penguins waddle up the beach, and their spectators try to be as quiet as possible.

# WE ARE FAMILY

## Do penguins have families?

Penguins make all kinds of nests to raise their families. Some hide among rocks or bushes, some stack up small pebbles and others snuggle down into piles of poop! Penguins don't nest at sea because there's no shelter out there. They *are* able to sleep while floating—which is pretty cool!—but they come ashore to breed and raise their babies. Both males and females make nests and both parents take care of the eggs and chicks.

## Bad habits

Male chinstrap penguins spend a lot of time stealing stones from other nests! In icy parts of Antarctica, stones can be hard to find. The males know that if they build the biggest nest of stones, a female might pick him as her partner.

## Daddy duties

After laying a single egg, female emperor penguins head to the ocean to rest and feed, while males stay with the colony. For three long, cold months, the males protect the egg, balancing it safely on their feet. When it gets really cold, the dads huddle together, shuffling to share body heat.

## Mom returns

Soon after the fluffy chicks hatch, female emperor penguins return from the sea. They are happy, healthy, and full of fish, ready to take over the babysitting duties. And now it's the males who take a long, hungry walk across the ice to go fishing.

## Pipsqueaks

Newborn penguins are very small. The smallest, little penguin chicks, weigh barely 1 ounce—not much more than a mouse! All penguin chicks eat a lot quickly to build up enough fat to keep warm and survive.

## Preschool

After a couple of weeks, young penguins start to hang out in groups called **crèches**. This helps them stay warm and safe while their parents are out fishing. It's probably a lot of fun for them too! Sometimes an adult or two will stay to keep the nursery safe.

# FEATHERY FUN

## Do all penguins look the same?

You might think all penguins have the same black and white feathers, but that is not true. Penguin chicks, with their fluffy, downy feathers, look completely different from adults. In fact, penguin chicks cannot even swim because their feathers aren't waterproof. They need to wait about four months for their adult feathers to grow in.

## All grown up

Adult penguin feathers are worth the wait! Short, wide, and tightly packed, they help penguins glide through the sea while keeping the water away from their skin.

## Hairy styles

As the chicks grow, their downy feathers are replaced by adult ones. This is called molting. At this stage, they look like scrawny teenagers with clumps of feathers coming away in patches. Try not to laugh at their funny beards and crazy haircuts!

## Fluffballs

Most penguin chicks are nice and fat under their first layers of soft gray feathers. These downy feathers protect them from the wind and cold, but still allow them to get heat from their parents' bodies.

### FIELD NOTES:
### HUMBOLDT PENGUIN

**LOCATION**
Chile and Peru

**HABITAT**
Rocky coasts

**HEIGHT**
25 inches

**FOOT COLOR**
Black

**FAVORITE SNACK**
Sardines

### Feather focus

Most birds molt a few feathers at a time over the year, but penguins lose them all at once! During this "catastrophic molt," penguins are not waterproof. So they sit still and focus all their energy on growing their feathers back!

### PENGUIN STYLE ICONS

Young penguins have a lot to look forward to—including the possibility that their adult feathers will give them a truly eye-catching look.

### Color combo

Rockhoppers are the rock stars of the penguin world. Not just for their cool spiky haircuts, but also for their red eyes, orange beaks, and pink feet. What a look!

### Fashion forward

Macaroni penguins are not named for the spaghetti-shaped feathers on their heads! "Macaroni" was an eighteenth-century nickname for men who wore big hairstyles! The sailors who first saw the penguins laughed at how they looked and the name stuck.

# DANGER ZONE

## Does anything eat penguins?

Sadly for penguins, the answer is yes. For many animals, the sight of a penguin means one thing: *lunchtime*! Whether on land or at sea, there any many different wild creatures that try to eat penguins.

### Escape tactics

The good news is that penguins are excellent swimmers and are often able to escape by moving quickly, leaping out of the sea and waiting on icebergs until the danger is clear.

### Bitesize

In Antarctica, most predators come from the sea, like leopard seals and orca. But penguins aren't safe on land, either—birds like skuas attack penguins from above, particularly the small and vulnerable chicks.

## Clever colors

The black-and-white patterns of a penguin protect them from getting spotted when they are swimming.

When a predator swims underneath a penguin, the penguin's white belly blends with the light sky above. This makes them hard to see.

When a predator swims above a penguin, their black backs merge with the darkness below.

This is called countershading, and it works sort of like camouflage.

## Don't feel too sad

It's important to remember that penguins are also expert hunters. They are big and scary predators if you happen to be a tiny fish! Even little penguins are sharp hunters who will gobble up as much food as they can catch.

## Hard time

In South Africa, there are sharks and sea lions in the sea that wouldn't mind eating a penguin sandwich. There are many dangers on the land there too—researchers have found that rats, cats, dogs, snakes, and even leopards have tried to make a meal of a penguin!

# PENGUIN TALES

## Why are penguins so popular?

All around the world, people just love penguins. From people who collect penguin stuffed animals to people who devote their careers to studying them; from chocolate cookies, cartoons, and movies to cozy pajamas and woolly hats . . . penguins are everywhere! And people have been telling stories about penguins for hundreds of years too.

## Māori mythology

The Māori of New Zealand have a name for the penguin that is known as the Fiordland penguin: *tawaki*. In the old legends, Tawaki was a god that walked the Earth in human form.

## Lightning legend

According to a Māori myth, people realized Tawaki was a god when he was spotted climbing a hill, removing his human clothes, and dressing himself in lightning. Can you see the similarity between the Fiordland penguin's striking yellow crest and a lightning bolt?

## Ancient explorers

Ngake and his wife Hinewaihua were Polynesian explorers in New Zealand a thousand years ago. They met many creatures that were new to them—seals (*kekeno*), dolphins (*aihe*) and little penguins (*kororā*)—and returned home to tell people there about these wonders.

## Ice icons

In 1911, explorer Herbert Ponting traveled to Antarctica. When he returned home he made "Ponko," one of the first penguin stuffed animals. Nowadays, a lady in Germany has the biggest collection of penguin toys in the world—with over 11,000!

## Penguin party

Penguins are so popular, they get two special celebrations every year: January 20 is Penguin Awareness Day and April 25 is World Penguin Day! You can join in the fun by having your own penguin party, or by helping raise money for conservation charities.

# SPACE PENGUINS
## Can technology help penguins?

Penguins are vulnerable because the climate is changing. Warming ocean waters are melting the sea ice where they live and breed. It is important to track how many colonies of penguins there are, so we can help them. Emperor penguins live in remote Antarctica, where the freezing temperatures make it very hard for scientists to study them. So, finding them from space could be the answer!

## Poop spotters

Scientists have found that it is possible to use satellites to spot groups of penguins from space. How do they do this? Well, by looking for giant stains on the ice caused by all their poop! These are called guano patterns.

## Big discovery

In 2018, using guano photos from space, a team of researchers found a previously unknown colony of more than 1 million Adélie penguins. They were living on remote islands off the coast of Antarctica called the Danger Islands.

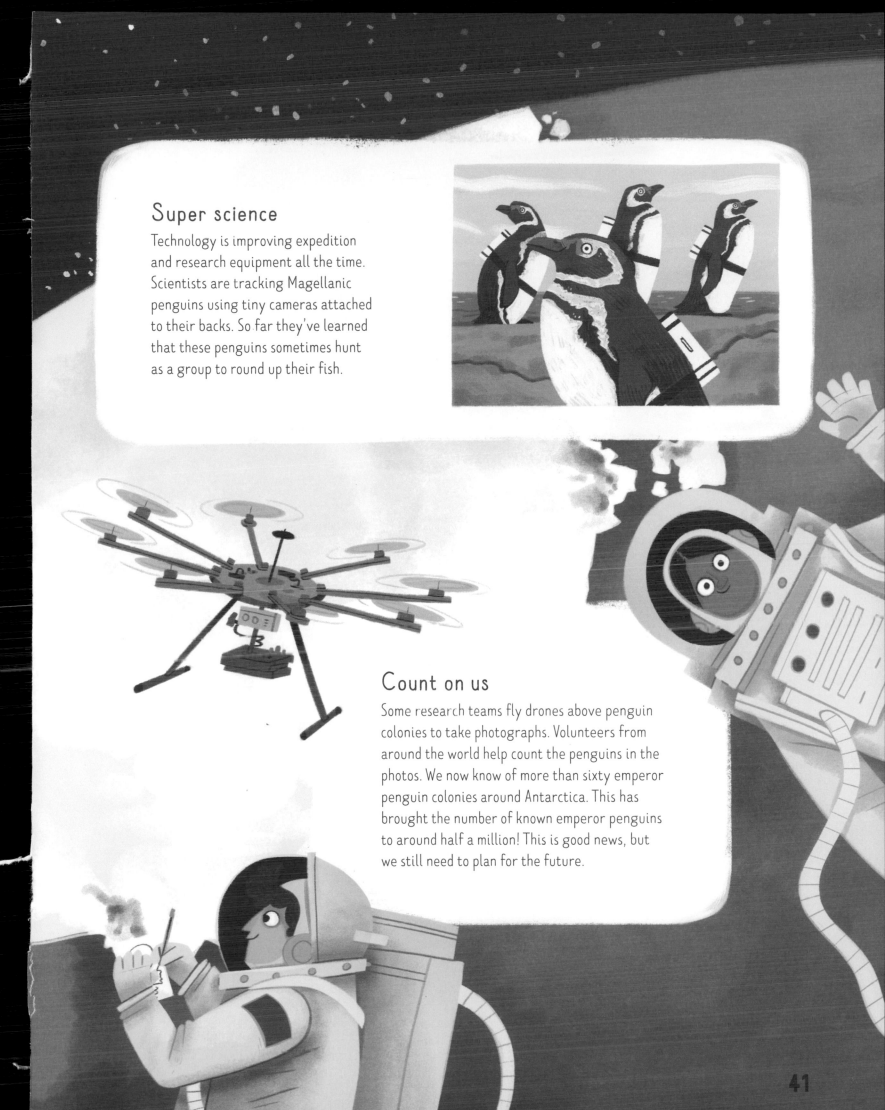

## Super science

Technology is improving expedition and research equipment all the time. Scientists are tracking Magellanic penguins using tiny cameras attached to their backs. So far they've learned that these penguins sometimes hunt as a group to round up their fish.

## Count on us

Some research teams fly drones above penguin colonies to take photographs. Volunteers from around the world help count the penguins in the photos. We now know of more than sixty emperor penguin colonies around Antarctica. This has brought the number of known emperor penguins to around half a million! This is good news, but we still need to plan for the future.

# WARMING WORLDS

## Will penguins go extinct?

Can you guess the most dangerous animal on the planet? It's us! All types of penguin have been affected by humans, and over the last fifty years, penguin numbers have been falling. These days, changes to the oceans are the biggest worry. In Antarctica, climate change threatens the future of animals across the whole food chain.

**EXTINCT PENGUIN**

**WAITAHA PENGUIN**
**LAST SEEN: 500 YEARS AGO**

The most recent species of penguin to go extinct was the Waitaha penguin. This happened about 500 years ago because of hunting by Polynesian settlers who had arrived in New Zealand.

**RAREST PENGUIN**

**GALÁPAGOS PENGUIN**
**JUST 1,200 LEFT**

Since the 1970s, the number of Galápagos penguins has fallen more than fifty percent. Humans brought pollution to the islands, but it is heat that is the biggest problem. When waters around the islands get too hot, it becomes hard for the penguins to find food.

## RARE PENGUIN

### YELLOW-EYED PENGUIN
#### JUST 4,000 LEFT

The yellow-eyed penguin—or hoiho, its Māori name—is in serious trouble. In New Zealand, their numbers have dropped over seventy percent in the last ten years. They live on predator-free islands, but are being caught in commercial fishing nets.

## A NEW PENGUIN?

### WHITE-FLIPPERED PENGUIN

Depending on which scientists you ask, this is either a new species or a sub-species of the little penguin. Around 5,000 of these "little white" or "white-flippered" penguins nest in New Zealand. They are unusual because they are truly nocturnal—they sleep in the day and are active at night. It's exciting to think a new species could be discovered today. But we need to protect them, because their numbers are also falling.

# LIVING TOGETHER

## Do penguins need our help?

I think we can agree that penguins are more than just cute! They are wild and wonderful and among the toughest animals on the planet. They have evolved over millions of years, but now their survival is in jeopardy. Humans are dangerous, but we have the potential to do important things. We must learn to coexist with other animals, take care of the environment and protect their habitats.

## Penguin rescue

In July 2000 there was a massive oil spill when a ship called *Treasure* sank just north of Cape Town, South Africa. Almost 20,000 African penguins were flown to safety. It was the largest penguin airlift in history!

## Good dogs

Middle Island, off southern Australia, used to be home to hundreds of little penguins. Sadly, red foxes from the mainland hunted them and almost wiped them out. At one point only four penguins were left! That's when local chicken farmer Swampy Marsh trained sheepdogs to protect the penguins. Thanks to Swampy and the dogs, there are now more than seventy little penguins on Middle Island.

## Protecting habitats

Penguins need healthy oceans but humans are clearing forests, polluting rivers and oceans, and changing the climate. We humans need to start rethinking the way we live! We can help penguins by working together to learn how to protect their habitats and live more sustainably.

## Join the count

You can help conservation efforts by counting penguins from your computer! Penguin Watch is a live-camera project on Zooniverse, a research platform. Log on today and start counting!

# PENGUIN WORDS

**CAMOUFLAGE:** A color or pattern that helps something blend into its surroundings.

**CIRCULATION:** The movement of blood around the body.

**CLIMATE CHANGE:** Long-term changes in global temperatures and weather patterns.

**COLONY:** A group of the same animals living together.

**CONSERVATION:** Protecting animals and nature.

**ENDANGERED:** May soon no longer exist.

**EQUATOR:** An imaginary line around the Earth that is the same distance from both North and South poles.

**EXTINCT:** No longer existing.

**FIELD NOTES:** A guide to identify wildlife in its natural environment.

**FOSSIL:** The shape of prehistoric plants or animals, preserved in rock.

**FROSTBITE:** An injury to part of the body from extreme cold.

**GLAND:** Part of the body that produces a useful substance.

**HABITAT:** The natural environment of animals and plants.

**HEMISPHERE:** Half of the Earth. The northern hemisphere is the half north of the **equator**, and the southern hemisphere is the half south of the equator.

**MIGRATE:** To travel to another place when the seasons change.

**MOLT:** To lose old feathers.

**PENINSULA:** A piece of land that sticks out into the water.

**PREDATOR:** An animal that kills or eats other animals.

**PREEN:** To neaten feathers.

**SPECIES:** A group of animals or plants that can breed together.

**STREAMLINED:** The perfect shape for moving quickly through water or air.

**TERRITORIAL:** Aggressive behavior when an animal feels that its territory is under attack.

**TERRITORY:** A space that animals defend from other animals.

# INDEX

For Nell, one day the Galápagos, promise. – Huw

For Ciara & Simone. – Sam

First published in the United States of America in 2023 by
Thames & Hudson Inc., 500 Fifth Avenue, New York, New York 10110

Library of Congress Control Number 2023930199

ISBN 978-0-500-65297-8

Printed and bound in China by C & C Offset Printing Co. Ltd

FSC
www.fsc.org

MIX
Paper | Supporting
responsible forestry
FSC® C008047

Be the first to know about our new releases,
exclusive content and author events by visiting
**thamesandhudson.com**
**thamesandhudsonusa.com**
**thamesandhudson.com.au**

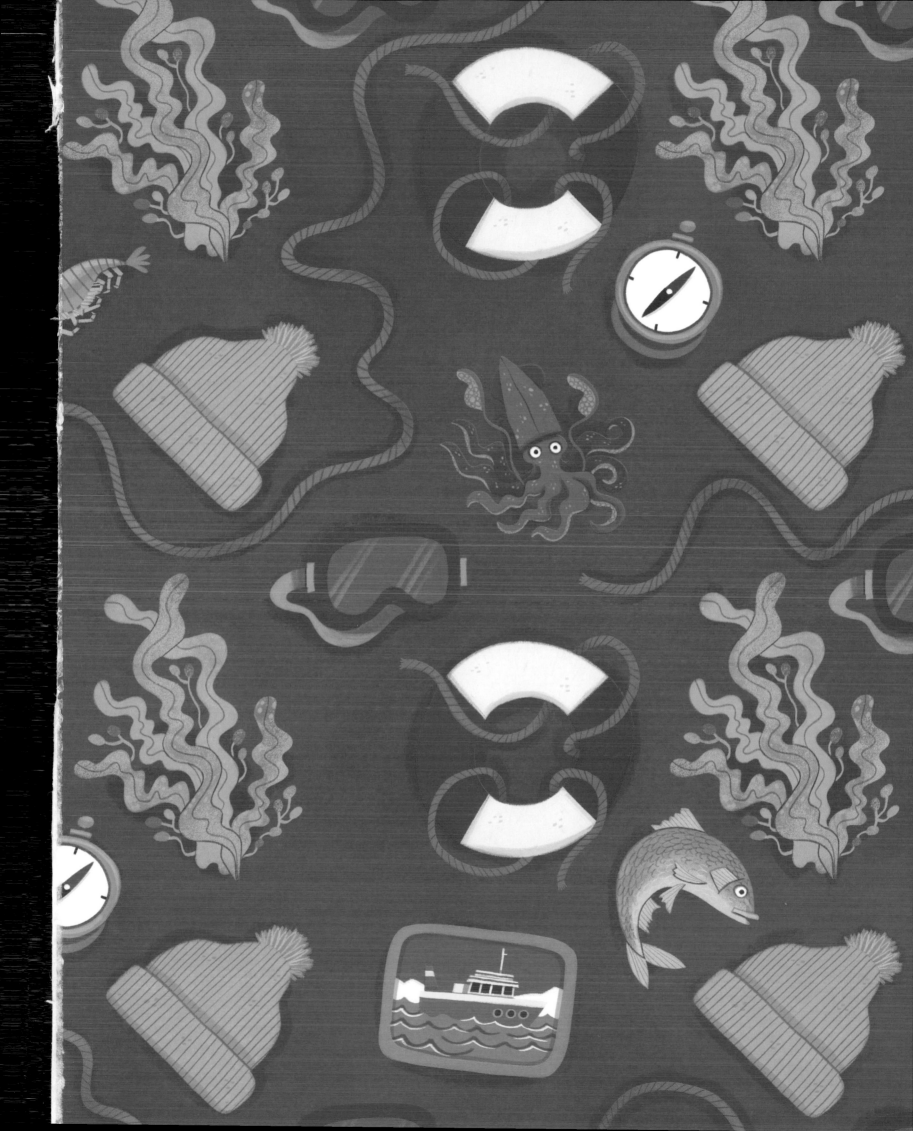